Go, Lovely Road

Series

Volume One

✣

Wild Flowers of the Holy Land

BY

MINNIE LOUISE RAUL

Formerly Minnie Louise Briggs

Author of "Famous Trees of the National Capital,"
Published, 1938 by The Sunday Star,
Washington, D. C.

✣

The Illustrations in This Book Are Reproductions
from Drypoint Etchings by the Author.

"Consider the lilies of the field, how they grow; they toil not, neither do they spin: And yet . . . even Solomon in all his glory was not arrayed like one of these."   (Matt. 6:28, 29)

Acknowledgments

My interest in this work began when I discovered a little book of pressed flowers tucked away on my library shelf. It had been presented to me many years ago by an aged friend, Mr. Owen T. Edgar. The volume was entitled "Pressed Flowers of the Holy Land", Pressed and Gathered in Palestine by Harry B. Green, 1898.

Then I began to visit libraries in quest of more information about the flowers of the Holy Land. Among the books I read, were Eleanor A. King's "Bible Plants for American Gardens", "Flowers and Trees of Palestine" by Augusta A. Temple, Giovanni Papini's "Life of Christ", "A Pilgrimage to Palestine" by Harry Emerson Fosdick.

I have kept a Nature Diary since early childhood with illustrations on each page. Using many of these sketches as studies for etchings, I now have more than 500 plates of Flowers, Trees and Nature Moods, which I am compiling into small volumes under the general title of "GO, LOVELY ROAD." This volume "WILD FLOWERS OF THE HOLY LAND is the first of the series.

The material relating to "Lily of the Field", "Star of Bethlehem" and "Cyclamen" is re-published here through the courtesy of *The Cathedral Age*.

M. L. R.

Go, Lovely Road

Go, Lovely Road, to the flowering Holy Land
Where the Wheat and the Tares o'er shadow the Rose.
Go through the meadows the Master once trod
Where the Iris and Tulips bloom purple and red
And the Lilies of the Field carpet the plain.

Go, Lovely Road, to the gentle slopes of Gallilee
Where shepherds pipe to their flocks on the hills,
Go where camels come laden with spices and myrrh,
Where the Fig, Olive and Vine grow by the way.

M. L. R.

Introduction

All summer, to the music of the wood thrush in my garden overlooking Georgetown, I spent working on a series of plates, printing some in colour, of the wild flowers of the Holy Land.

In great ecstasy I devoted myself to studying notes and making sketches, with books and botanies relating to Palestine and the open Bible by my side. I found the beauty of nature not only filled the Holy Land with colour but vividly served to illustrate the words of Jesus and the prophets.

Christians all agree that "the most important thing in life is to comprehend Jesus of Galilee. Whatever may assist in understanding His character and teachings is to be searched for with eagerness."

It is my sincere desire to offer a book presenting a few of the flowers found in this sacred land that will not only suggest the glory of this hallowed country to the reader's mind but will send more readers to the glorious scriptures.

From the Garden of Eden to the Holy Land came the brilliant anemones, the lupines, roses, lilies, buttercups and mallows and all the other exotic beauties, that cover in profusion the hills and plains of Palestine. This rich country that lies between the Syrian desert and the blue Mediterranean Sea is a narrow strip of land with a delightful climate where all plants grow, for the heat of the desert is tempered by the cool winds from the snow-capped mountains of Lebanon.

This land of the patriarchs, the nomad shepherds, of David and Solomon, and the prophets who walked and talked with God—and the ministry of Jesus—echoes with sacred history.

A narrow country, not more than 50 miles wide and 150 miles long, it is resplendent with flowers and shrubs, delicious fruits, "the olive, the fig and the vine," fragrant trees, cedars, frankincense, and myrrh, the blossoming herbs, cumin, dill and mint. There, too, are found the waving grains: barley, millet and wheat; hills carpeted with bright flowers and green valleys, bordered with the papyrus reed and rushes. All these have made a beautiful setting for the greatest story ever known.

In Bethlehem Jesus was born, laid in a manger of sweet hay, grass and flowers cut and dried in the sun, where the shepherds and the wise men came bringing gifts. Here he roamed as a boy. He saw the mustard grow tall and the lilies bloom in more splendor than the array of kings. He preached the Sermon on the Mount with words never heard before, with wild flowers blowing at his feet, here where the tares grow among the wheat and the golden mustards drop their tiny seeds.

Here in the spring, when the rains come, hidden seeds and shriveled bulbs burst into flower, carpeting the earth with a wealth of blooms so numerous it is impossible to identify them all. New species can be found at almost every step, over the rocky hillsides, in the cornfields, along the streams, among the reeds, rushes and sedges.

Jesus often chose the Jordan plain, studded with myriads of wild flowers, where camel and sheep graze, walking the winding paths from Jericho to Capernaum, rather than the mountain pass.

It is said that when they brought Him to Golgotha the earth darkened and the flowers of the earth trembled and stood still.

In preparing the etchings and making prints of wild flowers of the Holy Land, it seemed I walked with the Master among the flowers He loved over the hills of Galilee, where the shepherds piped to their flocks and the camels, with tinkling bells, laden with spices and myrrh, came up the valley.

The landscape of Palestine has changed little since Jesus' day. The olives still ripen under grey green leaves. The grapes turn purple on the vine. The lilies, red, yellow and blue, with the other brilliant flowers, still bloom in the fragrant grass.

M. L. R.

Contents

Lily of the Field — Anemone

Probably no flower is more loved or revered than the Poppy Anemone, so often called the "Lily of Palestine." From all the flowers of the field, Jesus chose this one to draw the lesson of implicit faith and the uselessness of worldly anxieties, one of the most beautiful illustrations in the Bible. (St. Matt. 6:28-30)

It matters not really which flower He meant, but botanists agree that it is the gaily coloured anemone, for they out-number the other floral beauties in the Holy Land, blooming luxuriantly and lavishly, crowding the valleys, climbing the hilltops, adorning the highways with gorgeous hues, bending among their fresh fern-like foliage on slender green stalks.

LILY OF THE FIELD
(Anemone)

9

Star of Bethlehem

Another of the most loved flowers of the Holy Land is the bright little Star of Bethlehem, whose face of six white pointed petals with a golden center gleams like a star in the swaying grass. It blooms in umbels of three or more among green leaves striped with white, six inches or more high; growing from bulbous root, it closes at sunset.

This delightful little blossom shines from large patches of gay anemones, Palestinian tulips, crowfoot, crimson adonis and the golden vetches in the early spring.

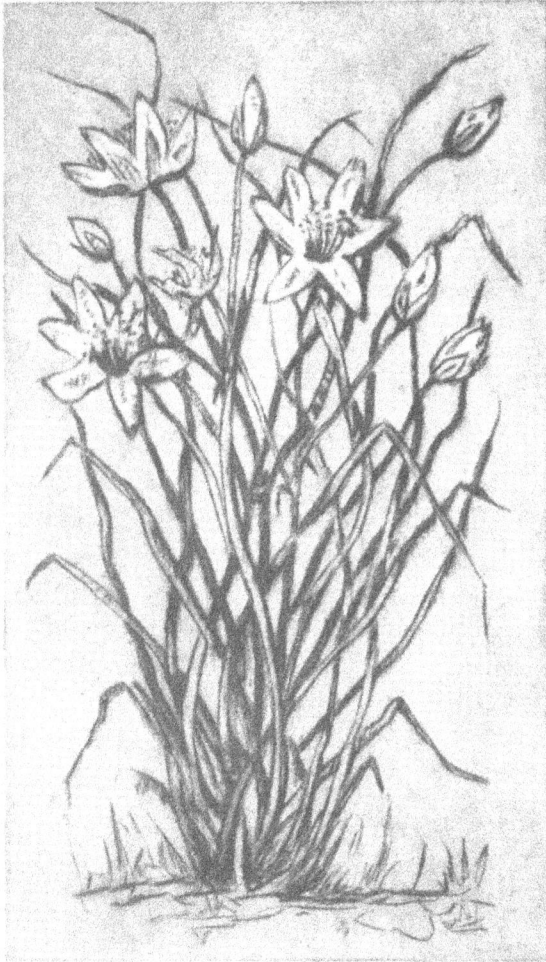

STAR OF BETHLEHEM

11

Crinkled-leaf Tulip

The Crinkled-leaf Tulip with its fine red-pointed petals and long twisted leaves grows a foot or more high along the rough stony paths of the hills and plains. The scarlet tapering petals have a fringed tip with a blackish spot at the base, surrounded by a yellow margin which adds much beauty to this handsome flower.

In this land of flowers, this clime where all plants grow, this oasis in the desert, where the mustard grows tall and the tares are found among the wheat, there is a special interest in the plants that grew upon the plains and on the mountains where our Saviour and His disciples walked. No flower more exotic grows in the Holy Land than the crimson crinkle-leaf tulip.

CRINKLED·LEAF TULIP

13

Wheat and Tares

Growing wild in the Holy Land, the neatly fashioned head and stalk of the Wheat nods among the darnel (the tares) and the thistle.

It is cultivated in Palestine and has been the chief food-grain since earliest times. Its gleaning, threshing and reaping are referred to repeatedly in the Bible, for Palestine produced wheat of very fine quality, "many eared and heavily bearded." Its blooming goes by scarcely noticed, but the ripened grain waving in the wind is like a sea of gold.

"When the blade was sprung up, . . . then appeared the tares also." (St. Matt. 13:26) The tares are poisonous but so like the wheat; they are difficult to detect until the wheat is gathered; however their grains are less crowded on the stalk. The tares were therefore left until the harvest. Then they were burned and the wheat gathered into the barns. Carrying away the chaff is a common scriptural reference. "The ungodly . . . are like the chaff which the wind driveth away." (Psalm 1:4)

The fields of Wheat and Tares beautify the fertile plains where the sword lily and other blossoming wildings add colour to the acres of green and gold.

WHEAT AND TARES

15

Pheasant's Eye

The Pheasant's Eye, or the Adonis Palestina, as it is sometimes called, is one of the many scarlet flowers that give the landscape of the Holy Land its brilliant hue. This beautiful little blossom has crimson petals around a golden center crowded with many stamens.

"The great Author of nature has not made a tint, a tiny hair or a grain of pollen without intent and meaning." Every flower is what it is in colour, form and odor to enable it to reproduce its kind and beautify the earth.

Mention of this flower goes back to the days of Canaan.

The eyes of the Saviour must have rested often on this lovely blossom, for it is very common in Palestine. It also grew around the threshing floors of the villages. It is much admired and loved by the people.

In the fall this wild flower may be found with crimson petals and dark centers.

PHEASANT'S EYE

17

Wild Mustard

In the land of exotic flowers of every hue the annual herb, Mustard, grows tall. The linnets and finches settle on the bending stalks, devouring the seeds of which they are so fond. (Mark 4:31, 32) Racemes of the pretty flower bloom and tiny seeds form and ripen as the golden petals fade and fall.

In another of the Master's parables, He selected this plant with its tiniest of all seeds to teach a lesson of faith and truth. (St. Luke 17:6)

"How often as He stood on a mountainside or on the shores of the Sea of Galilee, He illustrated His talks with the flowers and plants around Him."

WILD MUSTARD

19

Passion Everlasting

To add to the large number of scarlet flowers that cover the hills and plains of Palestine, the rosy, pungent Passion Everlasting peeps from the thorny underbrush, where it is usually found. The Holy Land is noted for its great number and variety of red flowers, a colour that is rare among wild flowers. Most prominent of these and one of the first to bloom is the anemone, thought to be "the lily of the field," then the large scarlet buttercup and the field poppy soon come to take its place; then the pheasant's eye and the scarlet passion everlasting.

This flower with its silver stalk and leaves, growing about a foot high, is seldom seen for it seems to delight in hiding beneath the thorns and thistles of the wildest parts of the Judean Mountains. The deep red clusters of florets are set in silver braces resembling moonlight.

Its colour and humble growth among the briars of the underbrush suggest the passion of our Saviour who walked the thorny paths. Thus came its name of Passion Everlasting.

PASSION EVERLASTING

21

Anise Flower

Among the many herbs mentioned in the Bible none is more exquisite than the cream colored Anise Flower. The seeds are valuable and used because of their aromatic and medicinal qualities.

Anise, mint, lavender, rue, hyssop, horehound, thyme, salvia, and rosemary, to name only a few of the aromatic herbs that were treasured in the Holy Land, were used as pot herbs as well as medicine. The seeds, leaves and stems of the anise were used also for tithes. (St. Matthew 23:23)

This plant, growing about a foot or more high with its parsley-like stem and leaves, adds a fragrant charm to the flowers massed over the plains and hills of Palestine.

ANISE FLOWER

23

Holy Thistle

The Holy Thistle, sometimes called St. Mary's Thistle, is a typical Bible plant. Probably it is called holy because it grew so plentifully in Palestine at the time of our Lord. The Holy Land abounds in a great variety of thorns, nettles and thistles.

In the Garden of Eden, God made everything that "is pleasant to the sight" and "good for food." After Adam's disobedience the ground brought forth thorns and thistles. (Genesis 3:18)

The holy thistle grows about four feet tall; it has an erect and branching stem. The red veined leaves are smooth above and downy beneath. The flower heads are sessile with rose-purple florets surrounded by spiny bracts.

HOLY THISTLE

25

Judean Clover

Over the hills and along the roadsides where divine feet have trod, trails the sweet vanilla-scented yellow Clover. It lifts its golden head from a branching stalk and fresh green leaves all over Palestine in the spring-time, to the rich enjoyment of the numerous sheep that graze there.

Despite the rocks and many pieces of broken walls and other structures, the flowers still bloom and among them is the fragrant Judean Clover, with its shamrock-like foliage. Upon close examination the flower heads are found to be round clusters of pea-like florets.

JUDEAN CLOVER

Madonna Flower

One of the most delicate of all plants of the Holy Land is the Madonna Flower. The lovely creamy blossoms and green feathery foliage well may suggest the gentle life of Mary, the Mother of Jesus. She must have admired and loved it, for it grew and blossomed among the more brilliant flowers near her home in Nazareth, and on the south ridges of Lebanon and over the plains.

The Madonna flower is composed of many tiny flowers with purple centers, not unlike our Queen Anne's Lace. Bracts radiate from the back of this handsome blossom, resembling rays as a halo.

Moses tells us Palestine was flowing with milk and honey—a land of rich pastures with many flowers. This description remains the same today, for everywhere are flocks of goats and sheep and herds of cattle grazing in rich green pastures. We are told that here the humming bee finds flowers from which to gather honey every month of the year. Among the wild flowers of every hue, none is so charming and beautiful as the Madonna Flower, which blossoms over the hills and on the plains of the Holy Land after the rains come in the early spring.

MADONNA FLOWER

29

Sword Lily
(Palestinian Wild Gladiolus)

Today, as in Bible days in Palestine, the number of wild flowers is so great that not even a modern botanist could clearly identify them all. One authority states that, among the more than 6,000 species named, about 400 peculiar to Palestine are found nowhere else.

Here among the larkspur, the crocus, the Turk's cap lily, the wild peony, jonquils, the violet and the rose, among the wheat and corn, on graceful stalk blooms the Sword Lily.

Its pink and purple blossoms hang loose in spikes, blooming only on one side of the stem, among long narrow leaves.

It is very abundant in the Holy Land along the roadsides and in the fields, especially in the corn fields. As one flower fades, another blooms.

SWORD LILY
(Palestinian Wild Gladiolus)

31

Cyclamen

The beautiful Cyclamen is another exotic plant whose fragrant flowers add beauty to the mass of colour spread over the Holy Land. It blooms among the mallows, hibiscus, mandrakes, and passion flowers high in the heights above Gethsemane, in the mountains and hills about Jerusalem.

It is one of the first flowers to bloom in the spring in Palestine, in colours from pure white to soft lavenders, pink, red, and purple.

The blossom with its wax-like petals turns down on the fleshy stalk among soft red-veined leaves.

CYCLAMEN

33

Millet

"The winter is past, the rain is over and gone"; (Song of Solomon 2:11) The ripening heads of Millet with broad green blades are very beautiful in the carpet of flowers that covers the Holy Land.

Millet is a grain that is widely cultivated in Palestine. "When it is green it is used as fodder. The grain is ground for bread when it is ripe."

The fields of the Holy Land are fully clothed in grass for a short time only, for after the rains cease and the hot sun shines upon the tender blades, the grains ripen and "The grass withereth, and the flower thereof falleth away:" (I Peter 1:24)

But, in the springtime, to see great patches of anemones, Palestinian tulips, crowfoot, crimson adonis, with the waving grasses, millet, wheat, barley and oats, in the fields or on the rocky hillsides is to see beauty beyond description.

MILLET

35

Long-leaf Iris

The Long-leaf Iris, whose slender leaves are taller than the flowers that bloom in racemes of two to four lilac-color blossoms to the stalk, is plentiful. These flowers as they fade turn to a yellowish henna shade and add more colour to the array of violets, roses, hyacinths, pinks and geraniums that burst into bloom in the early spring, when "the time of the singing of birds is come, and the voice of the turtle is heard . . . The fig tree putteth forth her green figs, and the vines with the tender grape give a good smell." (Song of Solomon 2:12, 13)

This beautiful iris blooms abundantly among the stones in dry places.

LONG-LEAF IRIS

Creeping Myrtle
(Periwinkle)

After the winter rains, the Creeping Myrtle, sometimes called Periwinkle, is another of the lovely flowers that grow among the mass of wild flowers. The soft blue flowers with white centers are very beautiful beaming from a density of dark green glistening leaves. (Ever-green)

There is another myrtle often spoken of in the Bible, a shrub or low tree that also has shining leaves, which was used for decoration. (Nehemiah 8:15) This shrub has a white flower bordered with purple, "which emits a perfume more exquisite than the rose." The modern Jews still adorn with myrtle the sheds and booths at the Feast of the Tabernacles. The seeds of this shrub, when dry, form our allspice. On Olivet grow the olive and the fig, and on some of the hills near Jerusalem is found the myrtle.

One of the loveliest flowers of Palestine is the blue blossom of the creeping myrtle found among the grasses, forming large blue patches, as its trailing vine runs over the ground.

CREEPING MYRTLE
(Periwinkle)

39

Thorny Burnet

Together with the crinkled leaf tulip, the long leaf iris, and the Palestinian lily on the stony hillsides grow many brambles, briars and burs and thistles. Among these is the Thorny Burnet that is thought to be one of the Christ thorns, of which the crown of thorns was made. (St. John 19:2)

The thorny burnet is a perennial with ascending spiked inflorescence. The fruit is small and apple-like among the dainty fern-like pinnacle leaves and long cruel thorns. It grows among the flowers of all species and is one of the armored plants that defend themselves with thorns, prickles and stinging hairs.

This is one of the thorns that "crackled under the pot" and is used for fuel.

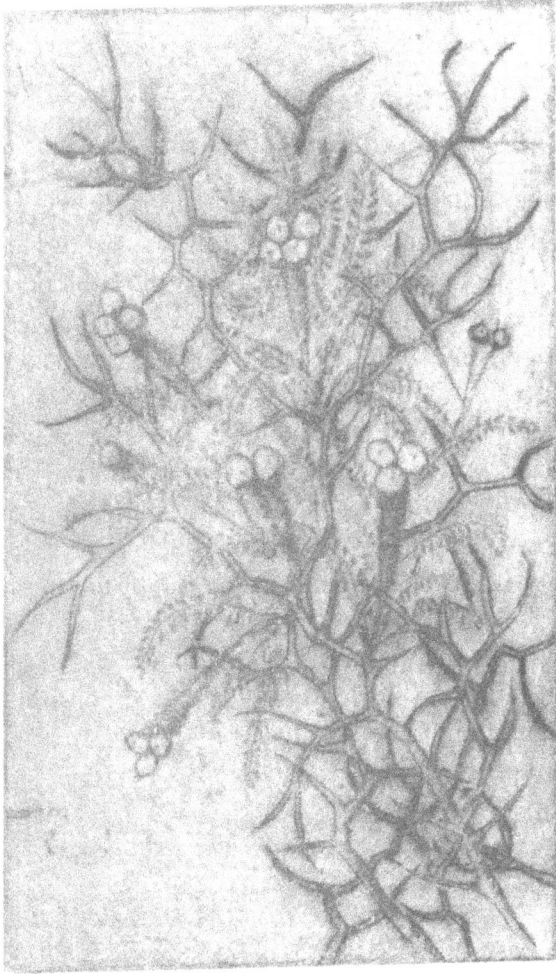

THORNY BURNET

41

Black Arum

One of the most stately and lovely flowers of the Holy Land is the Black Arum. It is a perennial herb, with an acrid root. It blooms over the hill country of Palestine in shady spots. The rich glossy leaves grow on long stems with blooms resembling our Jack-in-the Pulpit. The spathe is blackish purple within and green without. The spadix is a dark purple also and covered with tiny florets that ripen into a head of red berries.

According to an old legend the dark colour within the flower was received at the Crucifixion. Growing beneath the cross it is said that it caught the mysterious drops of agony which turned the blossom within a dark royal purple that has never blown away.

When the lovely flowers fade and droop, the seeds turn crimson and nod in the winds among the blossoms of autumn until winter comes.

BLACK ARUM

43

Wild Flax

Another of the wild flowers of the Holy Land that adds to the beauty of the field with its dainty pink, blue and lavender blossoms is the lovely Flax.

It is a well-known plant from whose fibres of the yellowish stem linen is woven. It is the earliest plant known to have been cultivated for spinning. In ancient times spinning was done by women of high birth and the fabric was worth its weight in gold.

The various processes employed in the manufacture of cloth included drying, peeling the stalks, separating the fibres, and hackling.

From the linen of the humble flax was made the grave cloth of Jesus. (St. John 19:40) Thus the fibre of the flax was put to a use that forever makes it sacred among the wild flowers.

WILD FLAX

Papyrus Reed

The tall graceful Papyrus Reed, the bulrush of the Bible, adds its beauty to the Holy Land's wealth of brilliant flowers. Its flowering head bends low with the wind along the water's edge.

Great masses of it grow in the plains of Sharon, along running streams, on the borders of lakes and pools along with other water-loving rushes and reeds. This plant has a blessed history. The first books of the Bible were written on papyrus paper, with a reed pen and with ink made from animal charcoal and oil. There is a strong link between the rushes and the recording of the Word of God. Our word, "Bible," comes from the Greek word, "Biblos," originally meaning papyrus. Papyrus paper was made by laying thin strips of reed side by side in opposite layers and gluing them together with a gum and then pressed paper-thin. The papyrus reed grows from about 6 to 16 feet tall. The blossoms of small spikelets droop on thread-like branchlets, forming a bushy crown that heads each angular stalk. The bending panicles of this reed Isaiah used to illustrate his lines, "to bow down his head as a bulrush." (Isaiah 58:5) In the story of the baby Moses, the Bible says "she took for him an ark of bulrushes, and daubed it with slime and with pitch, and put the child therein; and she laid it in the flags by the river's brink." (Exodus 2:3)

46

PAPYRUS REED

Passion Flower

The Passion Flower whose exquisite solitary blossom measures about two inches, blooms in pastel shades of pink, blue, lavender, yellow and white, in warm countries the world around. The fruit which turns yellow when ripe is edible. Botanists tell us there are 300 or more species of this flower.

Luxuriantly twining, climbing by long tendrils, it covers grass, shrub and tree. The blossom seems so mysterious and etherial that a legend has been woven about it. It is thought to be so symbolic of the Crucifixion as to be named the "Passion Flower," as the beautiful petals signify the faithful apostles; the stamen, the hammer; the anthers, the wounds in the feet and hands and side; the division of the pistil, the nails on the cross; the purple fringe growing from the center of the flower, the Crown of Thorns; the calyx, the glory of the halo; the leaves, the spears; and the tendrils, the whips and cords.

PASSION FLOWER

49

Dogwood

Among "The trees of the LORD" (Psalm 104:16), cypress, cedar of Lebanon, fir, date tree, and fig tree, are many blossoming shrubs. The rose bay, oleander, the red-bud, and the dogwood, to name only a few, give colour to the hillside of Palestine.

A very old and fanciful story has been told of the much loved dogwood which has a prominent place among the legends of flowers. At the time of the Crucifixion the dogwood was a huge tree growing among the other trees that covered the hills of the Holy Land. It grew so straight and strong that its timber was selected for the cross. The dogwood was said to be grieved over this cruel fate and our Lord seeing its sorrow, smiled upon it and said "Because of your regret for my suffering, never shall you grow large enough again to be used for a cross. Henceforth, you shall be low and twisted. Your blossoms shall be snow-white and form a cross, two long petals and two short ones. In the heart of each flower will be an image of the crown of thorns surrounded by a golden halo. In the middle of the edge of each petal there will be nail prints, brown with rust and stained with blood. The blossoms shall be as pure as my love for mankind, and they shall bloom within the reach of every one."

DOGWOOD

51

Selah *

"GIVE thanks unto the LORD; . . .
Sing unto him, sing psalms unto him:
talk ye of all his wondrous works." (Ps. 105:1, 2)
He sendeth the springs into the valleys,
which run among the hills . . .
He causeth the grass to grow for the cattle,
and herb for the service of man: . . .
The trees of the LORD are full of sap; . . .
Where the birds make their nests: . . .
He appointed the moon for seasons:
the sun knoweth his going down."

(Ps. 104:10, 14, 16, 17, 19)

SELAH

"For, lo, the winter is past,
  the rain is over and gone;
  The flowers appear on the earth;
  the time of the singing of birds is come, . . .
  The fig tree putteth forth her green figs,
  and the vines with the tender grape
  give a good smell." . . .

(S. of S. 2:11-13)

---

* Selah is used many times in poetical books of the Old Testament. According to Smith's Bible Dictionary it is thought to mean a pause in the singing voices, while the instruments perform alone; a term which had a meaning in the musical language of the Hebrew.

Selah

"O Lord, how manifold are thy works!
in wisdom hast thou made them all:
the earth is full of thy riches. (Ps. 104:24)

The grass withereth,
and the flower thereof falleth away:
But the word of the Lord endureth for ever.
(I Pet. 1:24, 25)

I will sing unto the Lord
as long as I live: . . .
My meditation of him shall be sweet:" . . .
(Ps. 104:33, 34)
The Bible

www.ingramcontent.com/pod-product-compliance
Lightning Source LLC
Chambersburg PA
CBHW081525040426

42447CB00013B/3342